To

____

From

____

Date

____

no worries

AN INSPIRATIONAL
MINDFULNESS JOURNAL

Studio 71 | DaySpring

INTRODUCTION

In Christ you were made to shine from the inside out. You were made to sparkle with joy, glimmer with hope, and point a light in His direction for anyone who wonders what glorious thing—or Person—you're so focused on. Of course, the enemy hates that! He tries everything in his (tired, overused, uncreative) strategy book to turn your eyes away from the beauty of following Jesus, toward the what-ifs and woes that worry the world every day. Since worries are emotional, it can feel so daunting to think about changing your thought patterns. So it's a very good thing that no one is asking you to do it alone.

On our own, stopping the worry train feels like an impossible feat of strength. But the Bible is full of proof and promises that worrying doesn't have to be a way of life for any of us. In Christ we have the tools we need to turn our attention toward everything good, true, lovely, excellent, and praiseworthy (Philippians 4:8). In Christ, we can say, "No worries"—not because we're perfectly worry-free, but because He invites us to submit every burden into His care and receive His peace instead. We become more of a conductor than a freight car, passing anything beyond our ability into His more than capable hands. That frees us up to enjoy the righteousness, peace, and joy of living in Christ. And that, friend, is a very worry-free life indeed.

HOW TO USE THIS JOURNAL

One of the best strategies for losing something we don't want is to replace it with something way better. This journal is designed to help you discover (or remember) the good qualities of God that far outweigh our reasons for worrying. Each week focuses on one reason *not* to worry:

Because His faithfulness is new every day

Because He takes your worries and anxieties

Because He is with you

Because He comforts you

Because He fights for you

Because He is able

Because He holds you steady

Because He knows better

Because He listens to you

Because He says not to worry

Each week includes a devotion to get you focused, then a Scripture, journaling prompts, and an activity for both the morning and evening of each day. As you choose to make God's Word your priority, and as you write down your thoughts each day, you will find a place to process and prepare your heart to grow closer to Him. Be intentional about releasing your worries to God each day. This will make room in your hands and heart for the good stuff—peace, thankfulness, and clear perspective.

WEEK 1

Great is Thy faithfulness,
great is Thy faithfulness
Morning by morning,
new mercies I see.
All I have needed,
Thy hand hath provided.

Great is Thy faithfulness, Lord, unto me.

GOD'S FAITHFULNESS IS NEW EVERY DAY

An old hymn with dated language captures a message your heart can still sing on a daily basis: God is faithful. Lamentations 3:22–23 puts it this way: "Because of the LORD's great love we are not consumed, for His compassions never fail. They are new every morning; great is Your faithfulness" (NIV). But is God's faithfulness real to you? Can you relate to the idea that He never lets us down?

What happens when that job change didn't work out quite the way you hoped? What if the baby you've been praying about for years hasn't come yet? Or the diagnosis isn't good? It can be so easy to attribute challenges to a God that drops the ball, drops our call, or simply has other things on His mind besides the things on our hearts.

The hymn and Scripture above both give a key to how we can view our dynamic with God.

Morning by morning, new mercies I see. God promises to be our Provider, Comfort, and Hope through life. Will you search for Him in the midst of it? We get to decide, whatever the situation, whether we'll focus on what we see or on what He says. Whether we'll dwell on the difficulties or on the One who is constantly guiding and strengthening us as we go.

His compassions never fail. They are new every morning. When we were kids playing softball in the cul-de-sac, we'd make a bad play and inevitably someone would yell, "Do-over!" Everyone would back up a few steps and start the play again, as if the error had never happened. The real world is different from neighborhood intramurals: We can't turn back time and erase the past. But we can, again and again, re-center our focus on the One who has infinite patience and strength. He never stops telling us, "My faithful love for you will never cease. Keep coming back. Keep trying. Keep looking for Me in the middle of it all...and I promise You, I will be found."

Morning Meditation

Give thanks to the Lord, for He is good!
His faithful love endures forever.

I CHRONICLES 16:34 NLT

List a few things you're thankful for today.

Scripture repeatedly tells us to live a life of thankfulness toward God. Do you find that easy or hard? Why?

What is one way that God shows His love for you?

Through prayer, invite God into your great moments and challenging moments today. Ask Him to draw your attention to His faithfulness and love toward you in every circumstance.

evening reflections

I do not hide Your righteousness in my heart;
I speak of Your faithfulness and Your saving help.

PSALM 40:10 NIV

How did you experience God's faithfulness today?

How did you see God's love at work today?

Did you talk about God with anyone today?

Before you go to sleep, text, email, or call someone to tell them of a blessing God has given you.

Morning Meditation

Because of the LORD's great love we are not consumed, for His compassions never fail. They are new every morning; great is Your faithfulness.

LAMENTATIONS 3:22–23 NIV

List a few things you're thankful for today.

How does it make you feel that God's compassion for you never fails?

Consider the verse from Lamentations above. Is there anything you need to release this morning in order to pick up His new mercies in the day ahead?

As you begin today, picture your worries and concerns as individual books lying out on a table. Name each book, then imagine closing it and putting it on the shelf. God will be your librarian today. No worries needed.

evening reflections

He will cover you with His feathers,
and under His wings you will find refuge;
His faithfulness will be your shield and rampart.

PSALM 91:4 NIV

How did you experience God's faithfulness today?

How did you see God's love at work today?

Imagine getting ready to zip yourself into a warm, comforting tent for the night. What worries or fears can you leave outside the tent?

Consider each of the worries you listed above
and ask the Lord to handle them while you sleep.

Morning Meditation

**Let love and faithfulness never leave you;
bind them around your neck,
write them on the tablet of your heart.**

PROVERBS 3:3 NIV

List a few things you're thankful for today.

What is a verse that holds significance for you?

Write out one of this week's Scriptures about God's faithfulness.

On a sticky note using a pen, or directly on your mirror using a dry-erase marker, write the above Scripture so you can memorize and meditate on it this week.

evening reflections

To the faithful you show yourself faithful;
to those with integrity you show integrity.

PSALM 18:25 NLT

How did you experience God's faithfulness today?

How did you see God's love at work today?

Do you find it easier to be kind to people who are kind to you? Do you get triggered when others are unkind?

Consider the interactions you had with people today and thank God for the ways He spoke in and through you.

Morning Meditation

The fruit of the Spirit is love, joy, peace, patience, kindness, goodness, faithfulness, gentleness, self-control; against such things there is no law.

GALATIANS 5:22–23 ESV

List a few things you're thankful for today.

Who is the Holy Spirit to you?

Name a situation you're in where you would like to have more of the fruit of the Spirit listed in Galatians 5:22–23.

Thank God for growing good fruit in you as you seek Him. Choose one aspect of the fruit above and ask Him to grow it further today.

evening reflections

All the ways of the LORD are loving and faithful toward those who keep the demands of His covenant.

PSALM 25:10 NIV

How did you experience God's faithfulness today?

How did you see God's love at work today?

Name a time in the past year when you saw the loving, faithful ways of God at work in your own life.

When we believe God, we tend to act on our beliefs. Consider some ways that you and God can make a difference together today.

Morning Meditation

Pursue righteousness, godliness, faith, love, endurance and gentleness. Fight the good fight of the faith.

1 TIMOTHY 6:11–12 NIV

List a few things you're thankful for today.

Which of the qualities listed in this morning's Scripture do you tend to notice in God's character? In what way?

Which of these qualities do you feel you need more of for a current situation you're facing?

When we pursue good things,
our worries tend to fade into the background.
Ask God to help you pursue the quality you wrote about today.

evening reflections

As for you, O Lord, you will not restrain your mercy from me; your steadfast love and your faithfulness will ever preserve me!

PSALM 40:11 ESV

How did you experience God's faithfulness today?

How did you see God's love at work today?

You are deeply loved by the Creator of the universe. How does this affect your perspective on life?

Spend at least five minutes on the floor, stretching. As you move your body, consider its uniqueness and abilities. Thank God for your body.

Morning Meditation

May Your faithful people rejoice in Your goodness.

II CHRONICLES 6:41 NIV

List a few things you're thankful for today.

When we faithfully choose Jesus every day, we can expect reasons for rejoicing! When was the last time you let out a big *whoop*?!

God is good, all the time! List three of your favorite ways of noticing His goodness.

Psalm 117:1 tells us to praise the Lord. The Hebrew word for "praise" here is shabach: to get loud! There are definitely times to shout to God in thankfulness. If you're feeling brave this morning, look over your list of reasons you're thankful and shout your praise to Him!

evening reflections

Into Your hands I commit my spirit;
deliver me, LORD, my faithful God.

PSALM 31:5 NIV

How did you experience God's faithfulness today?

How did you see God's love at work today?

When Jesus said the words of the Scripture above, He was on the cross demonstrating utter sacrifice. How are surrender and sacrifice powerful tools that God can use?

As you pray tonight, get on your knees and physically bow before God to show your surrender to Him.

Morning Meditation

He is the Rock, His works are perfect, and all His ways are just.
A faithful God who does no wrong, upright and just is He.

DEUTERONOMY 32:4 NIV

List a few things you're thankful for today.

Is there a worship song that resonates with you right now?

Who in your life needs to be reminded of God's strength and love?

*Speaking straight to ourselves sometimes yields important results.
Speak to your heart today about God's faithfulness.
Remind yourself, "I am not alone. The Lord is with me."*

evening reflections

The Lord is good; his steadfast love endures forever,
and his faithfulness to all generations.

PSALM 100:5 ESV

How did you experience God's faithfulness today?

How did you see God's love at work today?

How does God's unchanging, always-present, and reliable nature affect the amount of inner peace you feel?

Think back over the day—your conversations and situations—and look for God's presence in it all. Thank Him for being there.

Great is Thy faithfulness, Great is thy faithfulness

Morning by morning,

new mercies I see.

All I have needed,

Thy hand hath provided.

Great is Thy faithfulness,

Lord, unto me.

—THOMAS OBADIAH CHISHOLM

WEEK 2

Do not be anxious about anything,

but in every situation,
by prayer and petition,
with thanksgiving,
present your requests to God.
And the peace of God,
which transcends all understanding,
will guard your hearts
and your minds in Christ Jesus.

PHILIPPIANS 4:6–7 NIV

Have you ever felt a peace beyond what the situation called for? Maybe you've lost your child momentarily at the playground, but a calm settled over you before you saw her, along with the thought, *She must be out of sight for just a moment.* Maybe someone's job is on the line, but you instinctively know it's going to be okay. Or maybe, like Kay (below), a potentially life-threatening day became one where you could rejoice at God's desire to bring comfort.

Several years ago, someone mailed letters filled with a white substance to Kay's company. Spoiler alert: there was nothing harmful in them; it was just a cruel trick. But at the time, buildings were evacuated as 250 employees spilled into parking lots and awaited news of what was happening. From her seat on a curb, Kay's eyes were drawn up to the sky, which was bright blue and filled with puffy white clouds. She prayed, "God, is there anything to worry about?" She didn't hear an answer other than the deep, pure calm she felt. From that point on, she knew everyone was safe. She learned later that she herself had been one of the handful of employees who had been targeted with the letters. Even so, she felt a peace that surpassed what made sense. For Kay, peace led toward the person who had sent the letters, and forgiveness has led to a greater faith in God and who He is.

When the Bible commands something, we can be confident that God has equipped us to obey. So "do not be anxious" (Philippians 4:6) isn't just a pretty platitude, it's a possibility. Sometimes easier said than done, to be sure. But it's definitely attainable to lean into God's promise of peace as you ask Him for all that you need. Whatever you need to know of His character, He will show it. Whoever you need Him to be, He is. Trust, ask, and expect His very best, just for you.

Morning Meditation

We will receive from Him whatever we ask because we obey Him and do the things that please Him.

I JOHN 3:22 NLT

List a few things you're thankful for today.

How do you feel about asking God for things?

How do you feel about obeying and pleasing God?

Really pay attention to your needs today. Are they met? Where do you lack? Ask God to fulfill your every need.

evening reflections

When anxiety was great within me,
Your consolation brought me joy.

PSALM 94:19 NIV

How did you experience God's faithfulness today?

How did you see God's love at work today?

Did you have any anxious moments today? If so, how did you find your way out?

Spend time thanking God for the ways
He showed up for you throughout the day.

Morning Meditation

Therefore I tell you, do not worry about your life....

Are you not much more valuable than birds?

MATTHEW 6:25–26 NIV

List a few things you're thankful for today.

God promises to care for you even better than He cares for birds, which don't worry about anything. How does that encourage you?

What worries do you tend to carry with you?

Make a promise to God not to worry today. And anytime you notice those feelings, release them to Him—as many times as you have to!

evening reflections

Search me, O God, and know my heart;
test me and know my anxious thoughts.
See if there is any offensive way in me,
and lead me in the way everlasting.

PSALM 139:23–24 NIV

How did you experience God's faithfulness today?

How did you see God's love at work today?

Anxious thoughts are ones that don't carry the hope of Jesus in them. Is there an area in your life that is lacking hope?

Invite God to search your heart and heal those anxious thoughts.

Morning Meditation

So do not fear, for I am with you; do not be dismayed,
for I am your God. I will strengthen you and help you;
I will uphold you with my righteous right hand.

ISAIAH 41:10 NIV

List a few things you're thankful for today.

What is the difference between walking on a narrow surface alone, and walking on one while holding the hand of someone you trust?

Who in your life do you trust the most?

Be the steady hand to someone today,
and watch for those who act as a steady hand to you.

evening reflections

The Lord is my shepherd, I lack nothing.
He makes me lie down in green pastures,
He leads me beside quiet waters, He refreshes my soul.
He guides me along the right paths for His name's sake.

PSALM 23:1–3 NIV

How did you experience God's faithfulness today?

How did you see God's love at work today?

What's the difference between being the driver and being the passenger on a road you've never been on before?

As you pray tonight, determine to let God lead you tomorrow, from start to finish.

Morning Meditation

Worry weighs a person down;
an encouraging word cheers a person up.

PROVERBS 12:25 NLT

List a few things you're thankful for today.

How do you feel when someone dumps negative thoughts on you? How about when they compliment you or cheer you on?

How do you feel when *you* complain versus when you encourage or build someone else up?

At some point today, carry something heavy. It could be a five-pound bag of flour, a hand weight, or a child! Try to do it for at least five minutes. Then note how much better it feels to finally lay it down.

evening reflections

The LORD is my light and my salvation—whom shall I fear? The LORD is the stronghold of my life—of whom shall I be afraid?

PSALM 27:1 NIV

How did you experience God's faithfulness today?

How did you see God's love at work today?

Who made your day better? Who gave you a challenge?

As you lie down to sleep tonight, think of a person who has caused you worry or harm. Pray for them and ask God to give you His peace about the situation.

Morning Meditation

The LORD Himself will go before you.
He will be with you; He will not leave you or forget you.
Don't be afraid and don't worry.

DEUTERONOMY 31:8 NCV

List a few things you're thankful for today.

If you knew you had a strong, empowering, loyal bodyguard at your side, what would you be brave enough to try?

Do you know someone who could use a reminder of God's closeness today?

The Bible is full of promises of God's closeness and presence.
Use a Bible app, search engine, or Bible index
to find two or three more examples of His promises to be near.

evening reflections

I prayed to the LORD, and He answered me.
He freed me from all my fears.

PSALM 34:4 NLT

How did you experience God's faithfulness today?

How did you see God's love at work today?

Whose prayer life do you most admire?

Prayer builds your relationship with God, calms your fears, and it works! Decide tonight to connect with God in prayer every night throughout the rest of this journal.

Morning Meditation

Don't worry! I am Jesus. Don't be afraid.

MATTHEW 14:27 CEV

List a few things you're thankful for today.

Jesus is who He says He is, so you need not be afraid. What does that mean to you?

Fill in the lines below with things that worry you:
JESUS IS BIGGER THAN...

Text today's Scripture to a friend.

evening reflections

O God, listen to my cry! Hear my prayer! From the ends of the earth, I cry to You for help when my heart is overwhelmed. Lead me to the towering rock of safety, for You are my safe refuge, a fortress where my enemies cannot reach me.

PSALM 61:1–3 NLT

How did you experience God's faithfulness today?

How did you see God's love at work today?

Jesus is the Prince of Peace (Isaiah 9:7). How does knowing that you serve the Prince of Peace affect your everyday life?

As you settle in for sleep tonight, slowly and meditatively repeat "Jesus is my Peace" out loud at least ten times.

Morning Meditation

Tomorrow will worry about itself.

MATTHEW 6:34 NIV

List a few things you're thankful for today.

Think through the things on your mind this morning. Which ones can you affect today? Which things must wait for another day?

Deuteronomy 31:8 says that the Lord "goes before you." Knowing that He is fighting your battles today, which challenges can you leave in His care as you focus on more uplifting things?

Today, make a point of redirecting your thoughts toward the things that are within your control. Every time you catch yourself doing that, give yourself a point.

evening reflections

I will say of the Lord,
"He is my refuge and my fortress,
my God, in whom I trust."
PSALM 91:2 NIV

How did you experience God's faithfulness today?

How did you see God's love at work today?

Jesus left us with a gift of peace like no other (John 14:27). Do you believe it's possible to face challenges with a true sense of peace within?

How many points did you give yourself today?
Spend some time thanking the Lord for the ability to give Him your worries.

Do not be anxious about anything,
but in every situation,
by prayer and petition,
with thanksgiving,
present your requests to God.

and the peace of God, which transcends all understanding, will guard your hearts and your minds in Christ Jesus.

PHILIPPIANS 4:6–7 NIV

WEEK 3

So do not fear, for I am with you;

do not be dismayed, for I am your God.
I will strengthen you and help you;
I will uphold you with my righteous right hand.

ISAIAH 41:10 NIV

GOD IS WITH YOU

In one of the final scenes of the 1989 film *Indiana Jones and the Last Crusade*, Indy (played by Harrison Ford) stands at the edge of a canyon on a small ledge below a lion statue. On the other side of an uncrossable distance, he sees a small open door. The only thing he has at his disposal is this clue: "Only in the leap from the lion's head will he prove his worth." Indy is clearly shaken as he reviews his extremely limited options: turn around and face death, or step out into the abyss. He closes his eyes. Takes a wobbly breath. Lifts one leg high in the air—and falls forward. Instantly, his foot is stopped by a large beam that stretches from one side of the canyon to the other. Before that moment, the beam had been invisible. As soon as Indiana took a step of faith, he learned that support was there all along.

The image from that scene is such a poignant representation of taking God at His word. How often do we find ourselves poised at the edge of a figurative canyon, clutching a worn note with II Corinthians 5:7 written in bold letters: WE WALK BY FAITH, NOT BY SIGHT? We choose to believe God as we lift our trembling toes toward the unknown. And every time, God is there. It's His promise. To never leave or forsake us. To have our back, front, and sides. To gently lead and faithfully guide.

Trusting God means looking at the world through kingdom lenses. What we see might be fact, but what we know is truth. And the truth of God always trumps worldly knowledge or experience. Every time you find yourself facing down the unknown, remind yourself that you're not alone. You have the Creator and Sustainer of the universe showing the way.

Morning Meditation

The virgin will conceive and give birth to a Son,
and they will call Him Immanuel (which means "God with us").

MATTHEW 1:23 NIV

List a few things you're thankful for today.

What does God's nearness mean to you?

James 4:8 promises that if we draw near to God, He will draw near to us. What do you usually do to get closer to God?

Today, practice one of the things you just mentioned above.

evening reflections

You hem me in behind and before,

and You lay your hand upon me.

PSALM 139:5 NIV

How did you experience God's faithfulness today?

How did you see God's love at work today?

When was the last time you found yourself worrying over a "first world problem?" Did God show up for you? How?

Spend some time thanking God for His nearness today.

Morning Meditation

I am with you, and I will protect you wherever you go.... I will not leave you until I have finished giving you everything I have promised you.

GENESIS 28:15 NLT

List a few things you're thankful for today.

God's promises are so sure that He won't go anywhere until He delivers them all. What is something you've been praying and waiting for that you haven't seen yet?

What is a promise you've seen fulfilled in your life?

Before you start the day, text someone you care about to remind them of God's promise to fulfill His promises.

evening reflections

For me it is good to be near God; I have made the Lord God my refuge, that I may tell of all your works.

PSALM 73:28 ESV

How did you experience God's faithfulness today?

How did you see God's love at work today?

The people who know you best are the ones who have spent the most time around you. Likewise, the more time we spend with God, the more we know Him. Did you spend time with God today? What's something you gained from that time with Him?

Read Psalm 73 out loud as you settle down for the evening. As you read, pay specific attention to the differences between the people in the first half of the psalm and the author in the second half.

Morning Meditation

We walk by faith, not by sight.

II CORINTHIANS 5:7 ESV

List a few things you're thankful for today.

Walking by faith is a necessary part of following Jesus. In your own words, what does it mean to walk by faith?

Is it possible to walk by faith if we can see exactly where we're going? Why or why not?

Sometime today, choose two rooms in your home and walk from one to the other with your eyes closed. You walk by faith to the second room. You can't see it—but you know you'll get there.

evening reflections

Blessed are those You choose and bring near to live in Your courts! We are filled with the good things of Your house, of Your holy temple.

PSALM 65:4 NIV

How did you experience God's faithfulness today?

How did you see God's love at work today?

According to Scripture, we have full access to the good things of God's kingdom. List a few things you think that might include.

Galatians 5:22–23 lists nine things that those who seek God can expect to see growing in their lives. Read the passage and spend some time in prayer, asking to receive His good gifts.

Morning Meditation

Your own ears will hear Him. Right behind you a voice will say, "This is the way you should go," whether to the right or to the left.

ISAIAH 30:21 NLT

List a few things you're thankful for today.

How tuned in are you to God's voice?

God promises to speak when you need to hear Him. Name a recent time when you felt guided by His wisdom.

Spend some time thanking God for the way He speaks specifically to you. If you have trouble hearing Him, ask for Him to make His voice clear.

evening reflections

We thank You, O God! We give thanks because You are near. People everywhere tell of Your wonderful deeds.

PSALM 75:1 NLT

How did you experience God's faithfulness today?

How did you see God's love at work today?

How intentional are you about thanking God on a regular basis? Do you tend to live more thankfully, or more thanklessly?

Take five minutes to write down as many blessings as you can think of in your life.

Morning Meditation

No one will be able to stand against you as long as you live.
For I will be with you as I was with Moses.
I will not fail you or abandon you.

JOSHUA 1:5 NLT

List a few things you're thankful for today.

God promises that nothing is impossible with Him. Did you wake up knowing He's with you, or do you feel unsure?

What would you set your mind on today if you knew you couldn't fail?

First Samuel 17 tells of David, a young shepherd, and Goliath, a mighty warrior. Read David's story and imagine what it would have been like to face a giant with just a sling and a stone but knowing God is on your side.

evening reflections

Let me live forever in Your sanctuary,
safe beneath the shelter of Your wings!

PSALM 61:4 NLT

How did you experience God's faithfulness today?

How did you see God's love at work today?

When you picture resting under wings, what images and feelings come to mind?

As you settle in to rest for the evening, read and meditate on Psalm 91.

Morning Meditation

Once you were far away from God, but now you have been brought near to Him through the blood of Christ.

EPHESIANS 2:13 NLT

List a few things you're thankful for today.

Because Jesus paid the price for our sins, we can be close to God. What does Jesus' sacrifice mean to you personally?

How does your life now differ from your life before you accepted Jesus?

Ask God to bring you to someone who needs to hear the good news of Jesus today.

evening reflections

Those who know Your name trust in you, for you, O LORD, do not abandon those who search for You.

PSALM 9:10 NLT

How did you experience God's faithfulness today?

How did you see God's love at work today?

How has God made Himself known to you in your life? How has He made this personal?

Close your eyes and take a few deep, slow breaths. Imagine the warmth of God's embrace surrounding you.

Morning Meditation

He who sits on the throne will give them shelter. They will never again be hungry or thirsty; they will never be scorched by the heat of the sun. For the Lamb on the throne will be their Shepherd. He will lead them to springs of life-giving water. And God will wipe every tear from their eyes.

REVELATION 7:15–17 NLT

List a few things you're thankful for today.

God has already written the end of the story—and spoiler alert, He wins! (And so do we!) Knowing it ends triumphantly, how do your worries fit in?

All of your needs will be met. That's a promise. Write about a time you thought a "need" was actually a "want."

As you pray this morning, release your day and all its events into God's hands.

evening reflections

He will cover you with His feathers,
and under His wings you will find refuge;
His faithfulness will be your shield and rampart.

PSALM 91:4 NIV

How did you experience God's faithfulness today?

How did you see God's love at work today?

Did you notice anyone who needed a little extra love today? How did you treat the moment?

As you settle in for the evening, picture being enveloped in God's loving arms. Thank Him for that kind of comfort and protection.

So do not fear, for I am with you;

do not be dismayed,
for I am your God.
I will strengthen you
and help you;
I will uphold you
with My righteous right hand.

ISAIAH 41:10 NIV

WEEK 4

We can comfort

those in any trouble with the comfort
we ourselves have received from God.
For just as the sufferings of Christ
flow over into our lives,
so also through Christ
our comfort overflows.

II CORINTHIANS 1:4–5 NIV

GOD COMFORTS YOU

Has your car battery ever died? It worked just fine for the first 12,563 times you started the car, then suddenly you turned the key in the ignition and—*click*. Nothing. Mr. Battery had chosen not to answer your calls. He was corroded, or old, or just needed a charge. But at any rate, chances are you had no warning. And you may not have been in a convenient location when you needed to replace or repair the battery.

Dead batteries are among a million things that fall into the category of People Stuff. This is stuff that happens because we're human, and we live in a human world. It really has nothing to do with Providence shining down on you or Satan trying to ruin your day. Jesus said that in this world we *will* have trouble (John 16:33). Sometimes that means the small annoyances of living life on Earth. Yet even in those moments, God is ministering to us in loving, often subtle, ways. The Comforter, by His very name, comes to comfort us when we need it. If we didn't need Him, how would we ever know what comfort feels like?

If your battery died, maybe someone stopped to help you, or you had someone you could call. Maybe it died when you had nowhere important to go. Maybe batteries were on sale that day. Or maybe the roadside assistance person was the sort of individual who brightened your day. The Lord shows up in so many ways, and we're truly blessed when we open our hearts to see Him.

Not only will we personally grow in our awareness of God as we receive His comfort, but we'll have a gift to give others when they need it. God is the ultimate Giver, and He always gives us way, way more than we need just for ourselves.

Morning Meditation

Blessed be God, even the Father of our Lord Jesus Christ, the Father of mercies, and the God of all comfort.

II CORINTHIANS 1:3 KJV

List a few things you're thankful for today.

When you think of the word *comfort*, what images come to mind?

Big or small, what sorts of things have you needed comfort for lately?

Wear your most comfortable shoes today if you can.
Let them remind you to walk in the comfort of God.

evening reflections

May Your unfailing love be my comfort,
according to Your promise.

PSALM 119:76 NIV

How did you experience God's faithfulness today?

How did you see God's love at work today?

Think of someone who loves you. How does it feel to know that you are loved?

Wear your most comfortable pajamas to bed this week as a reminder to rest in God's comfort.

Morning Meditation

The Spirit of the Lord God is upon me;
because the Lord hath anointed me...to comfort all that mourn.
ISAIAH 61:1–2 KJV

List a few things you're thankful for today.

Jesus experienced such deep grief at times that one biblical writer referred to Him as "a man of sorrows." Have you experienced deep loss?

Have you invited Him in to comfort you in your most painful places?

Write out a loose agenda for the day.

evening reflections

Even though I walk through the valley of the shadow of death,
I will fear no evil, for You are with me;
Your rod and Your staff, they comfort me.

PSALM 23:4 NIV

How did you experience God's faithfulness today?

How did you see God's love at work today?

Sometimes God's boundaries and guidance are just what we need to help us feel secure. Do you find His boundaries to be comforting or constricting? Why?

If you are ready to open up to His love where you need it most, spend some time praying for His comfort in your pain. If you're not ready, ask Him to help you get to that point of trust.

Morning Meditation

We are confident that as you share in our sufferings, you will also share in the comfort God gives us.

II CORINTHIANS 1:7 NLT

List a few things you're thankful for today.

God's comfort is a sure thing. Where could you use a little extra reassurance of that today?

Read this morning's Scripture: Comfort is meant to be shared! Do you find it easy or hard to empathize with others?

Ask God to lead you to someone who could use some comfort and encouragement today.

evening reflections

Lord, You know the hopes of the helpless.
Surely You will hear their cries and comfort them.

PSALM 10:17 NLT

How did you experience God's faithfulness today?

How did you see God's love at work today?

What are you hoping for right now?

Spend some time thinking about how it will feel when what you hope for becomes reality. Thank the Lord for what He is doing for your future!

Morning Meditation

Now may our Lord Jesus Christ Himself, and God our Father,
who loved us and gave us eternal comfort
and good hope through grace, comfort your hearts
and establish them in every good work and word.

II THESSALONIANS 2:16–17 ESV

List a few things you're thankful for today.

What is most on your mind today?

What do you think God might be doing to help meet your needs?

Find someone to bless today.
"May God give you [peace, comfort, strength, wisdom, or whatever you know they need most], in Jesus' name." It may sound a bit awkward, but blessing others is one of the best gifts you can give.

evening reflections

You will increase my honor
and comfort me once more.

PSALM 71:21 NIV

How did you experience God's faithfulness today?

How did you see God's love at work today?

Sometimes prolonged challenges serve to grow and mature us. What is something you've been dealing with for a long time?

Spend some time thanking God for walking you through this time, and for what He is going to do to get you through.

Morning Meditation

I will turn their mourning into joy. I will comfort them and exchange their sorrow for rejoicing.

JEREMIAH 31:13 NLT

List a few things you're thankful for today.

Name something that God made beautiful after a difficult start.

Name something hard that you're facing today. How do you hope it ends?

Say this out loud: "God, I give You [today's hard thing]. What will You give me in return?" Leave it an open-ended question, and listen for a response throughout the day.

evening reflections

Send me a sign of Your favor.
Then those who hate me will be put to shame, for You,
O Lord, help and comfort me.

PSALM 86:17 NLT

How did you experience God's faithfulness today?

How did you see God's love at work today?

God can speak very personally to us, in ways that only we understand. How has He spoken to you?

Ask the Lord to send you a sign of His favor.

Morning Meditation

As a mother comforts her child,

so will I comfort you.

ISAIAH 66:13 NIV

List a few things you're thankful for today.

When you picture a mother comforting her child, what images come to mind?

How does it feel to be wrapped in someone's comforting arms?

If weather permits, wear a favorite sweater or scarf today to remind yourself of God's welcoming arms.

evening reflections

When anxiety was great within me,
Your consolation brought me joy.

PSALM 94:19 NIV

How did you experience God's faithfulness today?

How did you see God's love at work today?

List the things that weigh you down right now.

God cares when you struggle with anxiety and worry.
Ask Him to replace your anxieties with His consolation as you sleep.

Morning Meditation

Your love has given me much joy
and comfort, my brother.

PHILEMON 1:7 NLT

List a few things you're thankful for today.

Followers of Jesus have the unique ability to comfort and encourage one another. Who has been a source of comfort for you in the past?

When was a time you were able to comfort someone else?

Ask God to give you an opportunity to comfort or be comforted today.

evening reflections

I remember, LORD, Your ancient laws,
and I find comfort in them.

PSALM 119:52 NIV

How did you experience God's faithfulness today?

How did you see God's love at work today?

God's order of things is perfect, and is meant to bring us peace, comfort, and understanding. Think of one of the Ten Commandments (Exodus 20) and give a reason why this rule could be comforting.

Spend some time thanking God for His perfect order and plans for our lives.

We can comfort
those in any trouble
with comfort
we ourselves have
received from
God.

II CORINTHIANS 1:4 NIV

WEEK 5

The Lord your God
is he who goes with you
to fight for you
against your enemies,
to give you
the victory.

DEUTERONOMY 20:4 ESV

GOD FIGHTS FOR YOU

You're feeling pretty good about your Christmas décor this year. You know where the boxes are, you sorted through them last year to get rid of things you don't want anymore, and you know that a week or so after Thanksgiving you'll be ready to add some sparkle to your home. Then you start scrolling. And you see pictures of your friend's home, already glowing with red and green. You notice neighbors on ladders, stringing outdoor lights. You see styles and colors in stores, and you start wishing you had a whole new set of decorations...not to mention the pre-lit tree that would save you so much headache!

Nobody is trying to upstage you. They aren't more "right" than you. But somehow, seeing what others have going on can sometimes make you feel inferior, sad, or behind the times. The Bible reminds us that "our struggle is not against flesh and blood, but against the rulers, against the authorities, against the cosmic powers of this darkness, against evil, spiritual forces in the heavens" (Ephesians 6:12 CSB). Our thoughts and emotions often betray us. What's more, the enemy is out to discourage and defeat us in any way he can.

God doesn't always grab us by the hand and pull us away from the things that hurt us. But He doesn't leave us to struggle alone either. Instead, He prepares a table for us in the presence of our enemies (Psalm 23:5). In every situation, all the good things of His kingdom, like peace and joy, hope and contentment, are laid out before us. When we set our minds on Him and His goodness, we learn to love our life in Jesus. And we can celebrate with others in their happiness too. Your home and world can sparkle different from everyone else's—and be just as beautiful—*because God.*

Morning Meditation

The LORD stands beside me like a great warrior.
Before Him my persecutors will stumble.
They cannot defeat me.

JEREMIAH 20:11 NLT

List a few things you're thankful for today.

Are you more of an instant gratification or delayed gratification kind of person?

How do you usually feel if you don't see your preferred results right away?

Invite the Lord to lead your life today.
Ask Him what He wants to accomplish, and agree to follow His lead.

evening reflections

**You equipped me with strength for the battle;
you made those who rise against me sink under me.**

PSALM 18:39 ESV

How did you experience God's faithfulness today?

How did you see God's love at work today?

Was there a point today when you recognized that God had prepared you for the battle?

*Spend some time thanking God for
His protection and provision for the day.*

Morning Meditation

The Sovereign Lord is my strength;
He makes my feet like the feet of a deer,
He enables me to tread on the heights.

HABAKKUK 3:19 NIV

List a few things you're thankful for today.

What makes you feel mentally prepared for the day?

What makes you feel spiritually prepared for the day?

Spend a few minutes meditating on the above Scripture.
Write it down if you want, and work on memorizing it throughout the day.

evening reflections

The Lord is on my side; I will not fear.

What can man do to me?

PSALM 118:6 ESV

How did you experience God's faithfulness today?

How did you see God's love at work today?

As you look back over the day, were you hurt or offended by anything?

Consider the little hurts that may have happened today and forgive anyone who needs to be forgiven.

Morning Meditation

The Lord is good, a refuge in times of trouble.
He cares for those who trust in Him.

NAHUM 1:7 NIV

List a few things you're thankful for today.

How does it feel to know that God personally cares for *you*?

When you're in the moment, how do you remember that you have God to turn to in times of trouble?

Set your phone alarm to check in with God every hour today.
Evaluate how you've kept Him front of mind and
then invite Him once again to guide your next hour.

evening reflections

**The righteous person faces many troubles,
but the LORD comes to the rescue each time.**

PSALM 34:19 NLT

How did you experience God's faithfulness today?

How did you see God's love at work today?

Followers of Jesus can expect challenges on a regular basis. How have you seen God rescue you lately?

*Read Psalm 34 tonight before you go to bed.
Thank God for His faithfulness toward you.*

Morning Meditation

The joy of the LORD is your strength.

NEHEMIAH 8:10 NIV

List a few things you're thankful for today.

What do you do to keep a sense of humor?

Are you typically a glass-half-empty or glass-half-full kind of person? Why?

Do one thing that makes you smile big or laugh today.

evening reflections

Not by their own sword did they win the land, nor did their own arm save them, but your right hand and your arm, and the light of your face, for you delighted in them.

PSALM 44:3 ESV

How did you experience God's faithfulness today?

How did you see God's love at work today?

There's no doubt that we find ourselves battling at times. But even then, the Lord steps in to help. Name a time when you faced a fight and the results were miraculous.

Picture yourself as an armed soldier. Before you sleep tonight, picture removing each piece of armor and laying it down to rest. God will fight your battles as you sleep.

Morning Meditation

Come to Me, all you who are weary and burdened, and I will give you rest. Take My yoke upon you and learn from Me, for I am gentle and humble in heart, and you will find rest for your souls. For My yoke is easy and My burden is light.

MATTHEW 11:28–30 NIV

List a few things you're thankful for today.

When we feel exhausted and overworked, it's sometimes because we haven't let Jesus shoulder the load. Have you experienced emotional exhaustion?

Do you notice a difference when you take a step back emotionally and ask God to take the weight off your shoulders?

Make sure you're yoked with Jesus before you start the day.
Make a verbal commitment with Him,
and then intentionally rest your heart and mind in Him all day long.

evening reflections

The Lord is my strength and my shield;
in him my heart trusts, and I am helped;
my heart exults, and with my song I give thanks to him.

PSALM 28:7 ESV

How did you experience God's faithfulness today?

How did you see God's love at work today?

Have you noticed how praising God lifts your spirits? What other ways does praise benefit you?

Try it tonight—spend a few minutes just praising Him for who He is and what He does. Pay attention to how you feel before and after.

morning meditation

My grace is sufficient for you,
for My power is made perfect in weakness.

II CORINTHIANS 12:9 NIV

List a few things you're thankful for today.

Do you prefer to feel capable or dependent? What situations bring this out the most?

God honors our dependence on Him when we accept that we need Him. What's something you're facing today that you need Him for?

Today, thank God for something every time you catch yourself worrying.

evening reflections

I have set the LORD always before me;
because he is at my right hand, I shall not be shaken.

PSALM 16:8 ESV

How did you experience God's faithfulness today?

How did you see God's love at work today?

When you hear the term "right-hand man," what do you think of? Can you picture God, the Creator of the universe, as your closest helper?

Did anything "shake" you today?
If so, tell God about it and ask for His help.

Morning Meditation

Therefore, my dear brothers and sisters, stand firm. Let nothing move you. Always give yourselves fully to the work of the Lord, because you know that your labor in the Lord is not in vain.

I CORINTHIANS 15:58 NIV

List a few things you're thankful for today.

Who is the most courageous person you know? Why?

Whose faith do you most admire? Why?

Our emotions often alert us to a potential pitfall in faith. Anytime you feel unsettled, fearful, or worried today, take a step back and ask the Lord where you are wavering in trusting Him.

evening reflections

When the righteous cry for help,
the LORD hears and delivers them out of all their troubles.

PSALM 34:17 ESV

How did you experience God's faithfulness today?

How did you see God's love at work today?

Is there anything you want to cry out for help with tonight?

God promises to come to your aid when you need it.
Consider anything you're worried about tonight,
and reassure your heart that God is coming.

The victory belongs to the Lord.

PROVERBS 21:31 NLT

WEEK 6

**Humanly speaking,
it is impossible.
But not with God.**

Everything is possible with God.

MARK 10:27 NLT

GOD IS ABLE

In the 2015 movie *Little Boy*, Pepper (played by Jakob Salvati) is bullied and teased for believing that his dad will come home from war. He turns to a church leader for guidance—where he learns that "if you have faith as small as a mustard seed, you can say to this mountain, 'Move from here to there,' and it will move." In a moment of frustration on the playground, Pepper points boldly to a mountain in the distance and yells, "MOVE!" Of course, everyone laughs at him. But they stop laughing when suddenly an earthquake rocks the town. And a few days later, the local newspaper shakes the townspeople even more when they see the headline. Perhaps this boy's faith has moved mountains after all.

In a way, Pepper's sincere and innocent search for belief mirrors our own walk with Jesus. Not many people would look at the nearest mountain, command it to move, and expect results. But that's exactly the kind of faith we're called to. Do you believe in miracles? More importantly, do you believe in the Miracle Worker? A miracle, by definition, is simply a *wonder*—something that can't be explained in the natural sense. A diagnosis that healed on its own. A pregnancy that was deemed impossible. A happy "coincidence." Miracles make us think, and they test our sense of logic. Ultimately, they are meant to point to the One who can do the impossible.

With God, miracles are never in short supply. With God, the unlikely is hoped for and expected. What we see can shake us if we let it. But what we can't see should inspire us to dream big dreams—*with God*.

Morning Meditation

Not a single one of all the good promises the LORD had given... was left unfulfilled; everything He had spoken came true.

JOSHUA 21:45 NLT

List a few things you're thankful for today.

What do you think it means to have "faith like a child"?

In general, is childlike faith easy or hard for you?

Read Matthew 18:3, Mark 10:14, and Luke 18:17.
As you do, ask God to help you walk in childlike faith today.

evening reflections

My flesh and my heart may fail,
but God is the strength of my heart and my portion forever.

PSALM 73:26 ESV

How did you experience God's faithfulness today?

How did you see God's love at work today?

How did you operate in God's strength today?

If you're able, do five pushups (either from your toes or from your knees).
As you do, remind yourself,
"I am strong, but God is so much stronger than me!"

Morning Meditation

The grass withers and the flowers fall,
but the word of our God endures forever.

ISAIAH 40:8 NIV

List a few things you're thankful for today.

"Change is inevitable...but God never changes." How does knowing that God is a sure thing affect your willingness to step out in faith today?

Do you regularly spend time reading the Bible? Why or why not?

Read John 14:6, Isaiah 55:11, and Psalm 119:105.
As you do, ask God to remind you of a promise He will fulfill in your life.

evening reflections

Praise be to the Lord, to God our Savior,
who daily bears our burdens. Our God is a God who saves;
from the Sovereign Lord comes escape from death.

PSALM 68:19–20 NIV

How did you experience God's faithfulness today?

How did you see God's love at work today?

What burdens have you carried today?

Spend some time in prayer,
allowing God to bear those burdens for you. Sleep in peace.

Morning Meditation

God is not man, that he should lie, or a son of man, that he should change his mind. Has he said, and will he not do it? Or has he spoken, and will he not fulfill it?

NUMBERS 23:19 ESV

List a few things you're thankful for today.

Do you feel that God has ever let you down?

Is there anything you hold against God?

Depending on how you answered these questions, spend some time in prayer. Invite God to speak truth to your heart as you honestly share your feelings with Him.

evening reflections

The Lord God is a sun and shield;
the Lord bestows favor and honor; no good thing
does He withhold from those whose walk is blameless.

PSALM 84:11 NIV

How did you experience God's faithfulness today?

How did you see God's love at work today?

Picture God as the sun. What benefits and strength does the sun bring to the earth and to people?

Catch the sunset if you can.
Be outdoors this evening and enjoy the beauty of the Creator's rhythms.

Morning Meditation

I know that You can do anything,
and no one can stop You.

JOB 42:2 NLT

List a few things you're thankful for today.

What's in your plans for today?

Write down at least one thing you don't think you could manage today if God didn't intervene in His power.

Stand in front of the mirror and say out loud,
"In Christ I can do anything, and no one can stop me."

evening reflections

When He spoke, the world began!
It appeared at His command.

PSALM 33:9 NLT

How did you experience God's faithfulness today?

How did you see God's love at work today?

When we take God at His word, that is the very word that created the world! What burden or responsibility can you entrust to Him as you sleep tonight?

As you pray tonight, thank God for a few things
He created that are blessings in your life.

Morning Meditation

God is able to bless you abundantly,
so that in all things at all times, having all that you need,
you will abound in every good work.

II CORINTHIANS 9:8 NIV

List a few things you're thankful for today.

What does abundance mean to you?

What do you think it means to "abound in every good work"?

Picture a storehouse bigger than a football field. Imagine walking through it, knowing it is filled with every single tool and resource you need for this day. Pick out a few things to carry with you! What did you choose?

evening reflections

The Lord merely spoke, and the heavens were created.
He breathed the word, and all the stars were born.

PSALM 33:6 NLT

How did you experience God's faithfulness today?

How did you see God's love at work today?

Did anything happen today that was bigger than your control? Bigger than God's control?

As you wind down for the evening, intentionally turn your focus toward things that are bigger and more glorious than you: the stars, the compassion of others, or anything that reminds you of the breadth of God's sovereignty over life.

Morning Meditation

Now to him who is able to do immeasurably more than all we ask or imagine, according to His power that is at work within us.

EPHESIANS 3:20 NIV

List a few things you're thankful for today.

What are the biggest dreams on your heart?

Is it difficult for you to believe that God has more for you than anything you can think of or imagine? If so, what is holding you back from believing this truth?

Write your big dreams on sticky notes and place them where they will remind you of the unique wonder that God has created you to be. Then ask Him to have His hand on you as only He can.

evening reflections

He who dwells in the shelter of the Most High will abide in the shadow of the Almighty.

PSALM 91:1 ESV

How did you experience God's faithfulness today?

How did you see God's love at work today?

To abide is, in essence, to thrive in one place. Knowing you will thrive under God's care, write out a prayer of thanks for what God is doing in your life.

Remind yourself of the dreams you wrote on sticky notes this morning (or do that now if you haven't had a chance). Which one did you come closer to accomplishing today?

Morning Meditation

[Abraham] was fully convinced that
God is able to do whatever He promises.

ROMANS 4:21 NLT

List a few things you're thankful for today.

List a few concerns that are on your mind today.

Go over that list and write out what God might be able to do in each of those situations.

Fill in the blanks and say this out loud as often as you need today:
"I can't _______________, but God can _______________."

evening reflections

As for me, I am poor and needy,
but the Lord takes thought for me.
You are my help and my deliverer; do not delay, O my God!

PSALM 40:17 ESV

How did you experience God's faithfulness today?

How did you see God's love at work today?

God awaits your prayers and loves partnering with you. Are you satisfied with your current prayer life?

If you feel stuck in anything, ask the Lord to deliver you.
Then place your trust in Him to do it.

Everything is possible with God.

MARK 10:27 NLT

WEEK 7

You keep him
in perfect peace
whose mind is
stayed on you,
because

he trusts in you.

ISAIAH 26:3 ESV

GOD HOLDS YOU STEADY

Can you imagine the pressure of being seaweed? At one thousand meters below the surface of the ocean, the water pressure is one hundred times stronger than at sea level. And the ocean is, on average, almost four thousand meters deep! Seaweed tends to live at about the one-hundred-meter mark, because it requires sunlight for photosynthesis. Even at one hundred meters, though, the atmospheric pressure is ten times that of land. If it didn't have a strong anchoring system, seaweed would be uprooted and tossed along with the current. It would not survive at deeper levels. It needs to stay put. That's where *holdfasts* come in. Holdfasts are rootlike systems that dig in and keep seaweed from floating away. Spend a couple of minutes searching "seaweed holdfast" online, and you'll see what beautiful, complex structures they can be.

Similar to holding fast, *leaning* also requires the support of something strong. Whatever leans is dependent upon the thing against which it leans. Without strong support, the leaner doesn't *lean* at all—it *falls*. The beauty of the promise in Isaiah 26:3 is in its original word choice. We don't use "stayed" in common language today. But the original Hebrew for stayed in the above Scripture is *camak*, which means "to lean upon or take hold of." In other words, when our minds lean on God—when we turn our attention toward His unshakable Word and take hold of His unchanging truth—then supernatural peace awaits us.

When paired with Proverbs 3:5–6, the Bible makes it clear that we aren't designed to lean on our own understanding, but to place all our understanding in God alone. When we do, we are guaranteed not to be tossed about like seaweed in the current. We will stand firm in His peace.

Morning Meditation

Trust in the Lord with all your heart and lean not on your own understanding; in all your ways submit to Him, and He will make your paths straight.

PROVERBS 3:5–6 NIV

List a few things you're thankful for today.

List a few things you can control today.

List a few things that are out of your control.

As you pray this morning, submit your understanding—even the things you think you understand—into God's care.

evening reflections

What are mere mortals that You should think about them, human beings that You should care for them?

PSALM 8:4 NLT

How did you experience God's faithfulness today?

How did you see God's love at work today?

Did you catch yourself remembering to leave the unknowns to Jesus at any point throughout the day?

Thank God for the "wins"—any time you chose not to worry.

Morning Meditation

For I know the thoughts that I think toward you, saith the Lord, thoughts of peace, and not of evil, to give you an expected end.

JEREMIAH 29:11 KJV

List a few things you're thankful for today.

They say you devote the most thought to the things you care most about. Where are most of your thoughts going these days?

How much time do you spend planning and hoping for your future?

Take a moment to imagine what life would be like for you five years from now, if your bigger dreams came true.

evening reflections

Don't worry about the wicked or envy those who do wrong.
For like grass, they soon fade away.
Like spring flowers, they soon wither.

PSALM 37:1–2 NLT

How did you experience God's faithfulness today?

How did you see God's love at work today?

Did anyone hurt or offend you today?

Spend a few minutes forgiving the people you mentioned above. Forgiveness brings God's rest to your heart.

Morning Meditation

He who forms the mountains, who creates the wind, and who reveals His thoughts to mankind, who turns dawn to darkness, and treads on the heights of the earth—the LORD God Almighty is His name.

AMOS 4:13 NIV

List a few things you're thankful for today.

God will tell us what He's thinking—when it benefits us and when we ask. Do you know what He thinks of you?

Do you believe that God cares about you personally?

Ask the Lord what thoughts He would like to reveal to you today. Keep track of them throughout the day, and we'll take note of them this evening.

evening reflections

How precious to me are Your thoughts, God!
How vast is the sum of them!

PSALM 139:17 NIV

How did you experience God's faithfulness today?

How did you see God's love at work today?

Did you catch anything from God regarding His thoughts toward you?

If you understand anything fresh or important regarding His thoughts toward you, write those words on sticky notes and place them where you will see them throughout the week. Let the truth bless your soul.

Morning Meditation

Whatever is true, whatever is noble, whatever is right, whatever is pure, whatever is lovely...think about such things.

PHILIPPIANS 4:8 NIV

List a few things you're thankful for today.

How easy or difficult is it for you to think positively and hopefully? Write down a few Scriptures that you can recite to yourself when you find it difficult to see the light.

Are you surrounded by people who tend to think hopefully or more negatively?

Here's a challenge for you: destructive, or critical,
stop your thoughts and replace them with something good, true, or lovely.

evening reflections

When my anxious thoughts multiply within me,
Your comfort delights my soul.

PSALM 94:19 NASB

How did you experience God's faithfulness today?

How did you see God's love at work today?

What anxious or worrisome thoughts caught you up today?

Spend some time in prayer, releasing your anxieties to the Lord and asking Him to replace them with healing consolations.

Morning Meditation

Commit thy works unto the Lord,
and thy thoughts shall be established.

PROVERBS 16:3 KJV

List a few things you're thankful for today.

Which mundane tasks do you least enjoy doing?

Do you consider your daily work more of a job or a ministry? Do you believe it can be both?

God promises that when you work or give as though it's going straight to Him, there is huge blessing in it for you. Ask Him to help you keep a mindset of surrender and loving service in all that you do today.

evening reflections

O Lord my God...You have done great miracles for us, and we are ever in Your thoughts.

PSALM 40:5 TLB

How did you experience God's faithfulness today?

How did you see God's love at work today?

Do you believe God performs miracles on your behalf?

As you wind down this evening, spend some time recounting the good things that happened to you or around you today. Thank Him for each one.

Morning Meditation

As the heavens are higher than the earth, so are My ways higher than your ways and My thoughts than your thoughts.

ISAIAH 55:9 NIV

List a few things you're thankful for today.

In this week's story about leaning, we learned that we can anchor our minds in Jesus Christ. What do you think that means?

When something is anchored, is it better to leave it or to continually pull it out to readjust? Why?

This morning, picture a large filing cabinet labeled "For God." Imagine that anything you don't understand or can't solve has a file. Mentally look at each file and place it into the filing cabinet. Each time you find yourself worrying about something new today, "create" a new file and mentally put it away.

evening reflections

Be still in the presence of the Lord,
and wait patiently for Him to act. Don't worry about evil people who prosper or fret about their wicked schemes.

PSALM 37:7 NLT

How did you experience God's faithfulness today?

How did you see God's love at work today?

How good are you at waiting?

Before you sleep tonight, set a timer for three minutes. Sit in a comfortable position, close your eyes, and be still until the alarm goes off. It might seem like forever! But spend that time simply resting your mind and thinking about God and His goodness.

Morning Meditation

The word of God is alive and powerful.
It is sharper than the sharpest two-edged sword,
cutting between soul and spirit, between joint and marrow.
It exposes our innermost thoughts and desires.

HEBREWS 4:12 NLT

List a few things you're thankful for today.

List a few small things that are on your mind today.

Is reading the Bible a regular activity for you? Why or why not?

Commit today to reading something from the Bible every day for a week.
It could be one verse, one chapter, or more.
Just get yourself into the Word and experience it afresh.

evening reflections

Search me, O God, and know my heart:

try me, and know my thoughts.

PSALM 139:23 KJV

How did you experience God's faithfulness today?

How did you see God's love at work today?

Is it normal or unusual for you to make time to let God speak to your heart? How much time will you make for this today?

Spend some time in prayer tonight, but not to speak—to listen. Invite God to speak to you, and then sit expectantly. His voice doesn't always come as we expect, but He does love to communicate with us.

You keep him
in perfect peace
whose mind is
stayed on you,
because

*he trusts
in you.*

ISAIAH 26:3 ESV

WEEK 8

"My thoughts are nothing like your thoughts,"

says the LORD.
"And My ways are far beyond anything you could imagine."

ISAIAH 55:8 NLT

GOD KNOWS BETTER

Corrie ten Boom was a Dutch Christian survivor of the Jewish holocaust of World War II. She and her family were sent to work camps for hiding Jews and standing against the Nazis. For the rest of her life after the war, she wrote and spoke and traveled. Her message was to believers, calling them to big faith and big forgiveness. She spoke on resting in the Lord, working for Him without fear, and loving others no matter what.

Corrie and her father had a special relationship. He died in Scheveningen prison, before the family was sent to Ravensbrück work camp. Corrie often told stories that portrayed the wisdom her father had. One story she told occurred when Corrie was very little and worried about something. "'Corrie,' he began gently, 'when you and I go to Amsterdam—when do I give you your ticket?' I sniffed a few times, considering this. 'Why, just before we get on the train.' 'Exactly. And our wise Father in heaven knows when we're going to need things, too. Don't run out ahead of Him, Corrie.'"

Just as Corrie's father provided her with what she needed right when she needed it, God does the same for us. He knew about the details of today before He even invented "day" and "night." We think we know, but we don't—not really. Nothing is as sure as putting your hand in God's hand, letting Him lead you to the train station, and knowing that He has the ticket you need for whatever destination is next on your list. There is so much peace in trusting Him that way.

Morning Meditation

So do not fear, for I am with you; do not be dismayed, for I am your God. I will strengthen you and help you; I will uphold you with my righteous right hand.

ISAIAH 41:10 NIV

List a few things you're thankful for today.

It is said that the Bible tells us not to fear 365 times. Regardless of the actual number...it's a lot! Do you believe it's humanly possible not to fear?

Do you believe it's possible not to fear while holding God's hand?

Find someone to hug today. Make it a firm, strong hug! Remind them that they are held by God—and let that be a sweet reminder for you too!

evening reflections

True to Your word, You let me catch my breath
and send me in the right direction.

PSALM 23:3 THE MESSAGE

How did you experience God's faithfulness today?

How did you see God's love at work today?

How did God give you breathing room today? How did He allow you to shine?

Think through what's on your schedule for tomorrow.
Make sure to include something you are truly looking forward to.

Morning Meditation

Do not be conformed to this world, but be transformed by the renewing of your minds, so that you may discern what is the will of God—what is good and acceptable and perfect.

ROMANS 12:2 NRSV

List a few things you're thankful for today.

In a given week, how much time do you spend watching television, scrolling social media, or doing any other activity involving taking in information about the world?

In a given week, how much time do you spend exploring your interests and enjoying the people around you?

Decide what sort of balance you would like to have with the above activities, and commit to trying it for a week.

evening reflections

May all my thoughts be pleasing to Him,

for I rejoice in the LORD.

PSALM 104:34 NLT

How did you experience God's faithfulness today?

How did you see God's love at work today?

If your thoughts today were made public, how would you feel?

Submit your thought life to God in prayer tonight.
Ask Him to fill your dreams with reasons to rejoice.

Morning Meditation

We destroy arguments and every proud obstacle
raised up against the knowledge of God,
and we take every thought captive to obey Christ.

II CORINTHIANS 10:4–5 NRSV

List a few things you're thankful for today.

What do you think it means to take your thoughts captive to obey Christ?

Think of thoughts as visitors to your home. Negative ones knock on the door. Do you tend to let them in and entertain them? Or do you kick them off your property?

Draw an outline of a house on a piece of paper. Inside the house, write a few thoughts that you're going to allow to stay. Around the perimeter, write a few thoughts that are going to go straight to jail from now on.

evening reflections

You know when I sit down or stand up.
You know my thoughts even when I'm far away.

PSALM 139:2 NLT

How did you experience God's faithfulness today?

How did you see God's love at work today?

What are the benefits of knowing that God is fully aware of our thoughts and movements?

Take a blank piece of paper and write until it is filled. Write down everything on your mind tonight, good or bad. Offer your thoughts to the Lord and ask Him to be in charge of them while you sleep.

Morning Meditation

God did not give us a spirit of cowardice,
but rather a spirit of power and of love and of self-discipline.

II TIMOTHY 1:7 NRSV

List a few things you're thankful for today.

Imagine owning a car that you never got to sit in and drive. Would that seem strange? Those who love God have been given a spirit of power, love, and self-discipline. What do you think it means to "get in and drive" that spirit on a daily basis?

What do you think is happening when we operate in fear?

Picture putting on courage and strength like a warm coat on a cold day. Imagine that coat every time you do something brave today.

evening reflections

**Do not think of yourself more highly than you ought,
but rather think of yourself with sober judgment,
in accordance with the faith God has distributed to each of you.**

ROMANS 12:3 NIV

How did you experience God's faithfulness today?

How did you see God's love at work today?

It has been said that pride is a two-sided coin, where "I'm so good" is on one side and "I'm so bad" is on the other. Which side do you operate from more often?

Toss that coin of pride away and choose a new one, with sides that say "God is good" and "I am His." Trace a quarter onto a piece of paper, cut out two circles, write those words, and tape them onto each side. Place that quarter where you will be encouraged to see it.

Morning Meditation

Keep your heart with all vigilance,
for from it flow the springs of life.
PROVERBS 4:23 NRSV

List a few things you're thankful for today.

If you had a well, your only source of fresh and safe drinking water, what sorts of things would you do to protect what was inside?

What sorts of things would you want to keep out of the well? Why?

Invite God to examine your heart for any contaminants coming in or that have already seeped in. Ask Him for strategies to guard your heart with all vigilance.

evening reflections

Don't sin by letting anger control you.
Think about it overnight and remain silent.

PSALM 4:4 NLT

How did you experience God's faithfulness today?

How did you see God's love at work today?

Are you harboring any anger this evening?

Write down your concerns here and commit to leaving them alone until morning.

Morning Meditation

I pray that from His glorious, unlimited resources
He will empower you with inner strength through His Spirit.

EPHESIANS 3:16 NLT

List a few things you're thankful for today.

When you hear the words "inner strength," where do you believe that strength comes from?

What do you think are the limits of God's resources? Is there anything He doesn't have access to? Have you limited His access to anything in your life?

In what situations or areas of your life do you feel weakest? Write down your answers and, as you pray, ask God to provide the necessary strength for those things today.

evening reflections

I lie awake thinking of You,
meditating on You through the night.

PSALM 63:6 NLT

How did you experience God's faithfulness today?

How did you see God's love at work today?

Is it common for you to wake up at night? If so, what do you do with that time?

If you wake up at any point tonight, have a Scripture verse by your bedside that you can read and think about for a few minutes before you lay your head back down.

Morning Meditation

Let us think of ways to motivate one another to acts of love and good works.

HEBREWS 10:24 NLT

List a few things you're thankful for today.

Are there specific people in your life that you feel need to be encouraged today? Write their names below.

What types of things motivate you to do good deeds or share encouraging words?

Spend some time thinking of ways you can motivate the people around you today. Maybe you can post an encouraging Scripture on social media, or text a friend, or plan to "pay it forward" in the drive-through line. Be creative!

evening reflections

I will remember the deeds of the LORD;
yes, I will remember Your miracles of long ago.
I will consider all Your works and meditate on
all Your mighty deeds.

PSALM 77:11–12 NIV

How did you experience God's faithfulness today?

How did you see God's love at work today?

What is something the Lord did for you a year ago or more?

Before you sleep tonight,
tell someone of one good thing God did today.

"My thoughts are
nothing like Your thoughts,"
says the LORD.

*"And My ways
are far beyond
anything you
could imagine."*

ISAIAH 55:8 NLT

WEEK 9

This is the boldness
we have in Him,
that if we ask anything
according to His will,

He hears us.

I JOHN 5:14 NRSV

Imagine a busy mom. Maybe you *are* a busy mom, with kids and chores and work and errands—and all that goes into loving your family well. Now, imagine that one of this mom's sons comes to her and asks a question. Something like: *Mom, can I do the dishes tonight? Can I fold clothes and put them away? Can I please brush my teeth? Can you teach me to make my bed the way you do?* If she's a typical mom, these questions take her by pleasant surprise. And chances are, she will say yes. Why? Because she sees the maturity in her child's question. She understands that, with responsibility, he will grow, and that when he asks to do something kind, it will benefit everyone if she says yes. Depending on the age and experience of her son, it may take extra work on Mom's part to have "help" or to teach a new skill. But knowing her ultimate goal is to raise children who are capable and courageous, she leans into the opportunity.

Now imagine the same mom with the same kid. Today the son asks, "Mom, can I eat that ghost pepper?" Wisdom says Mom will put the brakes on that request.

In I John 5:14, when it says that God "hears" us, the Hebrew word is *akouo*, meaning "to give audience." In other words, when we ask something of God that He wants for us, then He will give us a place in His presence to ask. He doesn't ignore us or brush us off. He listens. So, how do we know what God wants? In the same way that a child knows his mom. He lives with her, spends time with her, and absorbs her words and behaviors like a sponge. As we stay close to God and pursue His heart, we get to know Him better. And He promises to shape our actual desires into the things that He wants for us (Psalm 37:4).

The Bible says that no promise of God goes unanswered. Spend time in the presence of God, and your heart will long for His promises and His truth. Then when you ask Him, He will hear you and answer with joy.

morning meditation

The eyes of the Lord are on the righteous
and His ears are attentive to their prayer,
but the face of the Lord is against those who do evil.

I PETER 3:12 NIV

List a few things you're thankful for today.

Write about a time when God answered your prayer.

How does it feel to know that God has His eyes and ears on you?

Set your mind on God today by reading Psalm 16:8.
For a little extra encouragement, write it out and carry it with you.

evening reflections

I cried out to Him with my mouth; His praise was on my tongue. If I had cherished sin in my heart, the Lord would not have listened; but God has surely listened and has heard my prayer. Praise be to God, who has not rejected my prayer or withheld His love from me!

PSALM 66:17–20 NIV

How did you experience God's faithfulness today?

How did you see God's love at work today?

Are you in a quiet season or a needy season? How does this season feel to you?

Invite God to show you more of who He is tonight. Ask Him to show you where you see Him incorrectly and to fill your thoughts with truth.

Morning Meditation

Ask, using My name, and you will receive,
and you will have abundant joy.

JOHN 16:24 NLT

List a few things you're thankful for today.

As you consider the things that worry you, what would you ask for in Jesus' name?

Are there areas in your life where you have joy now but didn't at some time in the past?

Read Romans 14:17 and carry its hope with you today.

evening reflections

You can be sure of this: The LORD set apart the godly for Himself.
The LORD will answer when I call to Him.

PSALM 4:3 NLT

How did you experience God's faithfulness today?

How did you see God's love at work today?

What do you think it means to be set apart by God?

Consider how you would feel if someone walked up to your spouse, child, or best friend and claimed that person as their own. You'd react, No, no, no! *That's how strongly God feels about you. Thank Him for setting you apart as His own.*

Morning Meditation

[God] listens to the godly person who does His will.

JOHN 9:31–32 NIV

List a few things you're thankful for today.

Do you believe that God truly wants to have conversations with you?

What do you think it means that God listens to you?

Do an Internet search for "the qualities of an active listener." Apply those to your prayer life with God today—believing that He loves listening to you as much as He enjoys talking with you!

evening reflections

I call on You, my God, for You will answer me;
turn Your ear to me and hear my prayer.

PSALM 17:6 NIV

How did you experience God's faithfulness today?

How did you see God's love at work today?

What's on your heart this evening? How would you like to pray?

Try to pray differently tonight, with full confidence that God hears you and wants to know your heart.

Morning Meditation

**In my distress I called upon the LORD; to my God I called.
From his temple he heard my voice, and my cry came to his ears.**

II SAMUEL 22:7 ESV

List a few things you're thankful for today.

Each day is a new chance to give God your concerns. Let's start this day fresh. What are you excited about?

What are you worried about?

Ask God if there's anything you need to fix or adjust in your thinking. Then spend a few minutes outside (or looking outside, if the weather isn't cooperating) with your favorite morning beverage and thank Him for a new day and new mercies.

evening reflections

In my distress I called to the LORD; I cried to my God for help.
From His temple He heard my voice;
my cry came before Him, into His ears.

PSALM 18:6 NIV

How did you experience God's faithfulness today?

How did you see God's love at work today?

This evening's Scripture looks like this morning's but is from another passage in the Bible. What does this say about continuing to come to God, again and again, as needed?

Sometimes praying silently just doesn't seem like enough for our aching souls. Tonight, try talking out loud to God as you would a dear confidant or spouse.

Morning Meditation

Since we know He hears us when we make our requests, we also know that He will give us what we ask for.

I JOHN 5:15 NLT

List a few things you're thankful for today.

It is said that God's answers are *yes*, *no*, and *not yet*. When an answer feels delayed to you, how are you at waiting?

Would you consider yourself a patient person? Why or why not?

Consider some things you've asked God for lately. Write them down somewhere and mark them as no, yes, *or* not yet. *If you're unsure, mark* not yet. *Set your heart to wait with trust, and not with a lack of confidence in His ability or willingness to move on your behalf.*

evening reflections

Praise the Lord! For He has heard my cry for mercy.

PSALM 28:6 NLT

How did you experience God's faithfulness today?

How did you see God's love at work today?

Can you think of a time when God has stepped in to prevent trouble for you or to change the course of events for the better?

Out loud, as if you are telling a story, share something that God has done for you (or do actually tell it to a friend or spouse). Remembering the past goodness of God is a great faith builder!

Morning Meditation

Then Jesus looked up to heaven and said,
"Father, thank You for hearing me. You always hear me,
but I said it out loud for the sake of all these people standing here,
so that they will believe You sent me."

JOHN 11:41–42 NLT

List a few things you're thankful for today.

Read Romans 10:17. What do you think it means to gain faith through hearing, and to gain hearing through the Word of God?

As you immerse yourself in the truth of Scripture, you will hear God's voice more clearly. What is something that God is showing you about Himself these days?

Find someone to encourage today by telling them about God.

evening reflections

The righteous cry out, and the Lord hears them;
He delivers them from all their troubles.

PSALM 34:17 NIV

How did you experience God's faithfulness today?

How did you see God's love at work today?

God listens closely to those who make it their purpose to get close to Him, listen, and follow His lead. When you face trouble, is it more normal for you to talk to friends first or to God?

Don't wait! If anything is on your heart tonight, take it straight to Him.

Morning Meditation

Then you will call on Me and come and pray to Me, and I will listen to You. You will seek Me and find Me when you seek Me with all your heart.

JEREMIAH 29:12–13 NIV

List a few things you're thankful for today.

One of the biggest facilitators of worry is when we try to solve things on our own, without the help of God. He also gives us Christian community to support us. Who in your life is part of your most trusted circle?

Write about a time when a friend or loved one supported you in a time of need. How about a time when you were that kind of support for someone else?

If you don't have the kinds of close friends you can turn to in trouble, ask God to bring someone your way, and consider joining a Bible study group either online or in your area. After all, He has designed us for community.

evening reflections

Even before a word is on my tongue, O LORD,
You know it completely.

PSALM 139:4 NRSV

How did you experience God's faithfulness today?

How did you see God's love at work today?

God knows you so intimately—but wants to hear from you anyway. You don't have to say things perfectly. Just tell Him what's on your mind this evening.

Before you go to bed tonight, consider who might benefit from hearing your voice. Text, call, or email in love.

This is the boldness
we have in Him,
that if we ask anything
according to His will,

He hears us.

I JOHN 5:14 NRSV

WEEK 10

Be strong and Courageous.

Don't be afraid or discouraged... for there is a power far greater on our side!

II CHRONICLES 32:7 NLT

GOD SAYS NOT TO WORRY

Eric Liddell was born in China and returned there as an adult missionary. That part of his life is a well-known and celebrated fact in heaven. But on earth, he is best-remembered as the Flying Scotsman. Eric was fast enough to win Olympic gold in the 400 meters in 1924. But he was dedicated enough to Jesus that he refused to run in his better race, the 100 meters, because it was held on a Sunday—his day of rest. Eric attributed his speed to the way God created him, and he ran for God's pleasure. Even so, he knew that being an athlete meant he would constantly need to be pushed past the limits of his understanding. To get faster and run more efficiently, Eric ran beyond his own ability. He once said, "The secret of my success over the 400 meters is that I run the first 200 meters as fast as I can. Then, for the second 200 meters, with God's help I run faster."

Like Eric Liddell, athletes know that they can probably do way more than they realize. But a good coach or trainer can see the ability and potential even better. A trainer's job is to convince an athlete to try, and try some more, until he or she sees what they're truly capable of. Experts say that at least half of athletic performance is mental—pushing past the voice in your head that says you can't, or you're tired, or you might fail. But chances are, if a wise trainer tells you to do a little more, it's because that person believes you have it in you.

As a follower of Jesus, God knows you have it in you to be bold and courageous. He knows you are capable of not worrying or harboring anxiety. He knows because He designed you. In the same way that Eric Liddell felt God's pleasure when he ran, you are meant to find enjoyment in your pursuit of God's purposes in your life. Freedom happens whenever we invite the Spirit of the Lord in (II Corinthians 3:17). Every time you take His path, you'll enjoy the freedom of life in Christ on whole new levels. It's a lifetime pursuit. But you never, ever run alone.

Morning Meditation

Peace I leave with you; My peace I give you.
I do not give to you as the world gives.
Do not let your hearts be troubled and do not be afraid.

JOHN 14:27 NIV

List a few things you're thankful for today.

How would you articulate the difference between the world's peace and God's peace?

What is needed in order to receive God's gift of peace?

Find a quiet place to sit and close your eyes for a few minutes. Hold your hands out in front of you, and tell the Lord you are ready to receive His peace.

evening reflections

The commandments of the LORD are right,
bringing joy to the heart.
The commands of the LORD are clear,
giving insight for living.

PSALM 19:8 NLT

How did you experience God's faithfulness today?

How did you see God's love at work today?

Do you believe that when God asks you to do something, it is for your benefit? Do you believe you are able to do what He asks? Why or why not?

Read Psalm 23 tonight before you sleep. Each night this week, we will focus on one verse of this chapter. This evening, speak verse 1 out loud and thank God for providing all your needs.

Morning Meditation

Give all your worries and cares to God, for He cares about you.

I PETER 5:7 NLT

List a few things you're thankful for today.

Each day is a chance for new worries to persist. God knows this! It's why He brings new mercies (Lamentations 3:22–23). List today's worries and cares.

Philippians 4:6–7 promises unexplainable peace when we submit our cares to Him. Have you experienced that kind of peace? Explain a time.

Take God at His word from today's Scripture. Give your worries and cares to Him in prayer, and thank Him for His care. Then step out in peace.

evening reflections

When anxiety was great within me,
Your consolation brought me joy.

PSALM 94:19 NIV

How did you experience God's faithfulness today?

How did you see God's love at work today?

How are you at intentionally resting or taking quiet time? Are you comfortable with the quantity and quality of your rest? How would you like to improve?

Read Psalm 23 and focus on verse 2. Take five minutes in a quiet place to meditate on the psalm and what kind of life God calls us to.

Morning Meditation

Let the peace of Christ rule in your hearts,
since as members of one body you were called to peace.
And be thankful.

COLOSSIANS 3:15 NIV

List a few things you're thankful for today.

Do you believe it's possible to "be thankful," even in challenging times?

What do you think it means to be peaceful toward one another? How should conflicts or differences be handled?

Is there anyone with whom you have a conflict right now?
Consider taking the next step toward reconciliation:
prayer, forgiveness, repentance, or reaching out.

evening reflections

I sought the LORD, and He answered me;
He delivered me from all my fears.

PSALM 34:4 NIV

How did you experience God's faithfulness today?

How did you see God's love at work today?

Use this space to release any fears you're dealing with this evening.

Read Psalm 23 and focus on verse 3. Different versions may use "soul" or "strength," but either way, God is the refresher. Invite Him to give you the refreshment you need tonight as you sleep.

Morning Meditation

Trust in the Lord with all your heart; do not depend on your own understanding. Seek His will in all you do, and He will show you which path to take.

PROVERBS 3:5–6 NLT

List a few things you're thankful for today.

Many of the verses this week focus on following God's direction. What do you think it means to be obedient to Christ?

Do you find it hard or easy to follow His lead? Which part is most challenging for you, and why?

Make "I trust You, God" your most-used phrase today. Speak it out as often as you remember. Try writing it on your hand or wearing a bracelet or other item that reminds you to declare your trust and let Him lead you.

evening reflections

When I am afraid, I put my trust in You.

PSALM 56:3 NIV

How did you experience God's faithfulness today?

How did you see God's love at work today?

What is one way, or one situation, in which you trusted God today?

Read Psalm 23 and focus on verse 4. What darkest valley have you experienced, and did you sense God's presence with you through it? Think of someone you know who may benefit from a reminder of His presence right now. Call them, or send them a text or email.

Morning Meditation

Therefore I tell you, do not worry about your life, what you will eat or drink; or about your body, what you will wear. Is not life more than food, and the body more than clothes?

MATTHEW 6:25 NIV

List a few things you're thankful for today.

What, if anything, are you worried about this morning?

Are there any "needs" you're concerned about that God has already promised to cover?

Read Psalm 91 as a reminder that God has you covered today.

evening reflections

I will rescue those who love me. I will protect those who trust in my name. When they call on me, I will answer; I will be with them in trouble. I will rescue and honor them.

PSALM 91:14–15 NLT

How did you experience God's faithfulness today?

How did you see God's love at work today?

Read Psalm 23 and focus on verse 5. When you think of a banqueting table set for you in the presence of your enemies, what do you think it represents?

The next time you encounter someone who is facing tough challenges, be generous and kind to them. Show them, through your actions, that the Lord hasn't forgotten them.

Morning Meditation

Do not be anxious about anything, but in every situation, by prayer and petition, with thanksgiving, present your requests to God.

PHILIPPIANS 4:6 NIV

List a few things you're thankful for today.

Are you facing anything new or intimidating today?

What about ongoing worries—on a scale of 1 to 10, how much are they bothering your thoughts today?

Imagine a vending machine where you insert coins to get something you're craving. This morning, let your worries be coins. After you deposit them all in God's hands, picture receiving peace like a warm cup of cocoa or a bag of your favorite treats.

evening reflections

Therefore we will not fear,
though the earth give way and
the mountains fall into the heart of the sea.

PSALM 46:2 NIV

How did you experience God's faithfulness today?

How did you see God's love at work today?

How does the verse above make you feel about any fears you may be facing right now?

Read Psalm 23 and focus on verse 6. Repeat this final verse a few times and remind your soul that God has more good planned for you than you'll ever be able to comprehend.

Morning Meditation

Don't worry about tomorrow,
for tomorrow will bring its own worries.
Today's trouble is enough for today.

MATTHEW 6:34 NLT

List a few things you're thankful for today.

Is there anything weighing on you that won't come to pass until tomorrow or later?

Can you think of someone you know whose outlook on life you admire? Describe some of their qualities that you appreciate. Contact that person today if you are able, or write a letter to them.

Determine to be the shining light of hope for someone today. Ask the Lord to put someone in your path. Then, when the opportunity presents itself, speak those words of kindness. Believe the best of that person. Help them in a way that only you can.

evening reflections

Give your burdens to the LORD, and He will take care of you.
He will not permit the godly to slip and fall.

PSALM 55:22 NLT

How did you experience God's faithfulness today?

How did you see God's love at work today?

What burdens do you have tonight that you can hand over to God before you sleep?

Read and recite all of Psalm 23 out loud.
If you haven't committed it to memory this week, write it out on a note card and determine to memorize this chapter to store it up in your heart, as Scripture suggests (Psalm 119:11).

Be strong and courageous.

Don't be afraid

or discouraged . . .

for there is a power

far greater on our side!

II CHRONICLES 32:7 NLT

The Comfort Promises by DaySpring™

No matter what you are facing today, you can rest in knowing the Creator of the universe loves you. He loves you deeply and perfectly with absolutely no conditions. And He's made hundreds of promises to you!

Below you'll find the 100 most referenced, quoted, and memorized Bible promises. At DaySpring, we call these *The Comfort Promises™*—the verses we turn to again and again for encouragement, joy, and strength.

For your convenience, we've provided a quick reference guide—a unique tool that makes it easy for you to find just the right comfort promises for your immediate need.

When you are AFRAID . . .

- He will not allow your foot to slip;
  He who keeps you will not slumber.
  PSALM 121:3 NASB
- Do not fear; I will help you.
  ISAIAH 41:13 NIV
- Draw near to God, and He will draw near to you. JAMES 4:8 CSB

When you are ANXIOUS . . .

- If you follow Me, you won't have to walk in darkness, because you will have the light that leads to life. JOHN 8:12 NLT
- Don't fret or worry. Instead of worrying, pray. PHILIPPIANS 4:6 THE MESSAGE
- He never changes or casts a shifting shadow. JAMES 1:17 NLT

When you need ASSURANCE . . .

- He is the faithful God, keeping His covenant of love to a thousand generations. DEUTERONOMY 7:9 NIV
- You're blessed when you're at the end of your rope. With less of you there is more of God. MATTHEW 5:3 THE MESSAGE
- He chose us...that we would be
  holy and blameless before Him.
  EPHESIANS 1:4 NASB
- You are saved by grace through faith...
  it is God's gift. EPHESIANS 2:8 CSB
- He cares about you. I PETER 5:7 NLT
- His divine power has given us everything required for life. II PETER 1:3 CSB

When you need COMFORT . . .

- The LORD is near the brokenhearted;
  He saves those crushed in spirit.
  PSALM 34:18 CSB
- Take delight in the LORD, and He will give you your heart's desires. PSALM 37:4 CSB
- My faithful love for you will remain.
  My covenant of blessing will never be broken. ISAIAH 54:10 NLT
- I have it all planned out—plans to take care of you, not abandon you, plans to give you the future you hope for.
  JEREMIAH 29:11 THE MESSAGE
- He will rejoice over you with gladness...
  He will delight in you with singing.
  ZEPHANIAH 3:17 CSB
- Blessed are those who mourn, for they shall be comforted. MATTHEW 5:4 ESV
- He comforts us in all our troubles
  so that we can comfort others.
  II CORINTHIANS 1:4 NLT
- God has chosen you and made you
  His holy people. He loves you.
  COLOSSIANS 3:12 ICB

When you need COURAGE . . .

- But You, LORD, are a shield around me, my glory, and the One who lifts up my head. PSALM 3:3 CSB
- I can do all things through Christ because He gives me strength. PHILIPPIANS 4:13 ICB
- He hears their cry for help and saves them. PSALM 145:19 CSB
- I will strengthen you, I will help you, I will uphold you with my righteous right hand. ISAIAH 41:10 ESV
- This is what the LORD says, he who made the earth, the LORD who formed it and established it—the LORD is His name: "Call to Me and I will answer you and tell you great and unsearchable things you do not know." JEREMIAH 33:2–3 NIV
- The LORD is good to those who wait for Him, to the person who seeks Him. LAMENTATIONS 3:25 NASB
- I will send you the Helper from the Father. He is the Spirit of truth who comes from the Father. JOHN 15:26 ICB
- He hears us. I JOHN 5:14 NASB

When you need HOPE . . .

- The LORD will fight for you, while you keep silent. EXODUS 14:14 NASB
- Be strong; don't give up, for your work has a reward. II CHRONICLES 15:7 CSB
- The LORD grants favor and honor; He does not withhold the good from those who live with integrity. PSALM 84:11 CSB
- He has planted eternity in the human heart. ECCLESIASTES 3:11 NLT
- His mercies never end. They are new every morning. LAMENTATIONS 3:22–23 CSB
- I am the living bread.... Whoever eats this bread will live forever. JOHN 6:51 NIV
- Anyone who believes in Me will live, even after dying. JOHN 11:25 NLT
- We have this hope as an anchor for the soul, firm and secure. HEBREWS 6:19 NIV

When you need JOY . . .

- Do not grieve, for the joy of the LORD is your strength. NEHEMIAH 8:10 NIV
- You will fill me with joy in Your presence. PSALM 16:11 NIV
- You turned my lament into dancing. PSALM 30:11 CSB
- Give, and it will be given to you. LUKE 6:38 NIV

When you are LONELY . . .

- He will be with you; He will not leave you or abandon you. DEUTERONOMY 31:8 CSB
- The LORD your God is with you wherever you go. JOSHUA 1:9 CSB
- He Himself has said, "I will never leave you or abandon you." HEBREWS 13:5 CSB

When you are feeling OVERWHELMED . . .

- For nothing will be impossible with God. LUKE 1:37 ESV
- The God of all grace...will himself restore, confirm, strengthen, and establish you. I PETER 5:10 ESV

When you need PEACE . . .

- The LORD gives His people strength; the Lord blesses His people with peace. PSALM 29:11 CSB
- Peace I leave with you. My peace I give to you. JOHN 14:27 CSB
- God's peace will keep your hearts and minds in Christ Jesus. PHILIPPIANS 4:7 ICB

When you need PROTECTION . . .

- You are a hiding place for me; you preserve me from trouble. PSALM 32:7 ESV
- You protect people as a bird protects her young under her wings. PSALM 36:7 ICB
- God has not given us a spirit of fear, but one of power, love, and sound judgment. II TIMOTHY 1:7 CSB
- Humble yourselves before the Lord, and He will lift you up. JAMES 4:10 NIV

When you need ENCOURAGEMENT . . .

- His faithful love endures forever. PSALM 100:5 CSB
- I will be your God throughout your lifetime—until your hair is white with age. ISAIAH 46:4 NLT
- I will give you a new heart and put a new spirit within you. EZEKIEL 36:26 CSB
- For I am convinced that neither death nor life, neither angels nor demons, neither the present nor the future, nor any powers, neither height nor depth, nor anything else in all creation, will be able to separate us from the love of God that is in Christ Jesus our Lord. ROMANS 8:38–39 NIV
- He will not let you be tempted beyond your ability. I CORINTHIANS 10:13 ESV
- He has created us anew in Christ Jesus, so we can do the good things He planned for us. EPHESIANS 2:10 NLT

When you need FORGIVENESS . . .

- I will forgive their sin and will heal their land. II CHRONICLES 7:14 NIV
- Though your sins are scarlet, they will be as white as snow. ISAIAH 1:18 CSB
- By giving Himself completely at the Cross, actually dying for you, Christ brought you over to God's side and put your lives together, whole and holy in His presence. COLOSSIANS 1:22 THE MESSAGE
- He...will forgive us our sins and purify us. I JOHN 1:9 NIV
- God, who...will bring you with great joy into His glorious presence without a single fault. JUDE 1:24 NLT

When you need GUIDANCE . . .

- He will make your paths straight. PROVERBS 3:6 CSB
- The LORD will continually guide you. ISAIAH 58:11 NASB
- When the Spirit of truth comes, He will guide you into all truth. JOHN 16:13 NLT

When you need HEALING . . .

- He heals the brokenhearted and binds up their wounds. PSALM 147:3 ESV
- By His wounds we are healed. ISAIAH 53:5 NIV
- I will give you back your health and heal your wounds. JEREMIAH 30:17 NLT

When you need HELP . . .

- I will send you rain in its season, and the ground will yield its crops and the trees their fruit. LEVITICUS 26:4 NIV
- Day after day He bears our burdens. PSALM 68:19 CSB
- He will give His angels orders...to protect you in all your ways. PSALM 91:11 CSB
- The LORD will guard your going out and your coming in from this time forth and forever. PSALM 121:8 NASB
- He is a shield to those who take refuge in Him. PROVERBS 30:5 CSB
- A stronghold for the poor...a refuge from storms and a shade from heat. ISAIAH 25:4 CSB
- No weapon turned against you will succeed. ISAIAH 54:17 NLT
- He will strengthen you and protect you. II THESSALONIANS 3:3 NIV

When you need REST and RENEWAL . . .

- The LORD is my shepherd, I lack nothing. He makes me lie down in green pastures, He leads me beside quiet waters. PSALM 23:1–2 NIV
- He renews my life; He leads me along the right paths for His name's sake. PSALM 23:3 CSB
- He satisfies you with good things; your youth is renewed like the eagle. PSALM 103:5 CSB
- Those who wait for the LORD will gain new strength; they will mount up with wings like eagles, they will run and not get tired, they will walk and not become weary. ISAIAH 40:31 NASB
- Come to me, all who labor and are heavy laden, and I will give you rest. MATTHEW 11:28 ESV
- The Son of Man came to find and restore the lost. LUKE 19:10 THE MESSAGE
- Jesus answered, "Everyone who drinks this water will be thirsty again, but whoever drinks the water I give them will never thirst. Indeed, the water I give them will become in them a spring of water welling up to eternal life." JOHN 4:13–14 NIV
- Our inner person is being renewed day by day. II CORINTHIANS 4:16 CSB
- If anyone is in Christ, he is a new creation. II CORINTHIANS 5:17 CSB

When you need STRENGTH . . .

- He gives power to the weak and strength to the powerless. ISAIAH 40:29 NLT
- The Spirit helps us in our weakness. ROMANS 8:26 ESV
- He will keep you strong to the end so that you will be free from all blame on the day when our Lord Jesus Christ returns. I CORINTHIANS 1:8 NLT

When you are SUFFERING . . .

- He will sustain you; He will never allow the righteous to be shaken. PSALM 55:22 NASB
- As a father has compassion on his children, so the LORD has compassion on those who fear Him; for He knows how we are formed, He remembers that we are dust. PSALM 103:13–14 NIV
- I will be with you.... When you walk through the fire, you will not be scorched. ISAIAH 43:2 CSB
- I will be your God throughout your lifetime—until your hair is white with age. ISAIAH 46:4 NLT
- The LORD is good, a stronghold in the day of trouble. NAHUM 1:7 ESV
- Remain in Me, and I will remain in you. JOHN 15:4 NLT

When you need WISDOM . . .

- Continue to ask, and God will give to you. Continue to search, and you will find. Continue to knock, and the door will open for you. MATTHEW 7:7 ICB
- It is because of Him that you are in Christ Jesus, who has become for us wisdom from God—that is, our righteousness, holiness and redemption. I CORINTHIANS 1:30 NIV
- Now if any of you lacks wisdom, he should ask God...and it will be given to him. JAMES 1:5 CSB

When you are WORRIED . . .

- Your Father knows the things you need before you ask Him. MATTHEW 6:8 ICB
- God will meet all your needs. PHILIPPIANS 4:19 NIV

First Edition, July 2022

Published by:

DaySpring

Published by DaySpring, 501 Nelson Place, Nashville, TN 37214, USA. DaySpring is an imprint of HarperCollins Christian Publishing, Inc.

HarperCollins Publishers, Macken House, 39/40 Mayor Street Upper, Dublin 1, D01 C9W8, Ireland (https://www.harpercollins.com)

Written by: Trieste Vaillancourt
Cover Design by: Lorianne Boyd
Illustrations by: Stephanie Henry and Amber Maine
Lettering by: Shelby Thompson
Designed by: Jessica Wei

ISBN: 978-1-64870-634-9

Printed in Vietnam
26 27 28 29 30 QPV 8 7 6 5 4